HOLY TRINITY OF CHILES

A BOOK OF POETRY
BY
SCOTT CAPUTO

BLUE LIGHT PRESS ❖ 1ST WORLD PUBLISHING

1st WORLD
PUBLISHING

SAN FRANCISCO ❖ FAIRFIELD ❖ DELHI

HOLY TRINITY OF CHILES

Copyright ©2010 by Scott Caputo

1ST WORLD LIBRARY
106 South Court Street
Fairfield, Iowa 52556
www.1stworldpublishing.com

BLUE LIGHT PRESS
1563 45th Avenue
San Francisco, California, 94122

BOOK AND COVER ART / DESIGN
Melanie Gendron
www.melaniegendron.com

FIRST EDITION

LCCN: 2010930702

ISBN: 9781421891514

Poems in this collection have appeared (some in earlier versions), or will soon appear in the following journals and periodicals:

Bay Area Seasonal Review: "The Spanish Masters"
Bellowing Ark: "Walking Home from the Library"
Haight Ashbury Literary Journal: "The Same Day"
Mobius: "Letter to Andrea"
Poetry Explosion Newsletter: "Man of Loaves", "Touch"
Poetalk: "The Spanish Masters","Yesterday's Newspapers"
Poetry Motel: "traffic city blues"
Red Owl: "The Fountain of Youth"
Red Rock Review: "Day of the Dead", "The Last Hour Before Midnight"
Ruah: "El Santurio de Chimayo"
Saranac Review: "Hiroshima Museum of Art"
Sensations: "Postcards", "Holy Trinity of Chiles"

ACKNOWLEDGMENTS

I want to thank my beautiful wife, Melissa, for her love and support;
I would like to thank my parents, Steve and Sharon Caputo, for their love and encouragement;
Diane Frank, for being such a great poetry teacher and for pushing me hard to make this the best book possible;
Max and Pam Noyes at *M. Coffee* in Half Moon Bay, and Kit Kennedy at *Gallery Café*, for sponsoring my poetry readings;
Doug and Margaret Stow at the *Paper Crane* in Half Moon Bay, for creating such beautiful broadsides of my work;
All my friends at the Half Moon Bay poetry readings, including Bob and Sherri Rose-Walker, Richard and Vicki Lawson, and Ken Paul Lozada, for making poetry so much fun;
Matt Gabrielson, for being such an encouraging first poetry teacher;
Kirston Koths, John Doiron, Jeremiah Loverich and all the members of the Poets Across the Bay writer's group, whose feedback I have valued so much.
Julie Morrison and Carrie Powell, for their encouragement during my early poetry years; and finally, my manuscript readers, who gave me such helpful feedback: Diane Frank, Kirston Koths, Tom Amsberry, John Doiron, Paul Ellis, Julie Morrison, John Rowe, Doug and Margaret Stow, and Sherri Rose-Walker.

CONTENTS

I. TAPAS AND APÉRITIF

II. PICNIC UNDER TREES

III. Cinnamon and Pepper Chai

IV. Bread from the Oven

V. Berry Lemon Trifle

How small that is, with which we wrestle,
what wrestles with us, how immense;
were we to let ourselves, the way things do,
be conquered thus by the great storm —
we would become far-reaching and nameless.

—Rainer Maria Rilke "The Book of Images"

I. Tapas and Apéritif

HOLY TRINITY OF CHILES

While Columbus was busy
spreading Christianity in the new world,
the natives were teaching his men
the holy trinity of chiles.
They were surprised at the flavors of
chocolate, cherries, and tobacco
merging with a fiery hotness
that made their mouths glow
all night like votive candles.
This Jesus, who ate with tax collectors,
sat with these people to eat meat in molé sauce.
True confessions poured out with cleansing sweat;
their watery eyes turned heavenward.
Shrines were replaced with churches,
bland food with tongues of flame.
As the believer grows in faith,
the chile matures from green to red,
the ribs infused with fire of spirit
to be shared with the world.
Unlike Christianity,
this great evangelization of the chile
took only a century to reach China
and the remote forests of Hungary,
the tongue infinitely easier to convert than the heart.

DAY OF THE DEAD

I awaken to the smell of incense and fresh bread.
I push up out of the ground like a flower of bones.
Following the scent, I see my face on an altar of marigolds.
I'm smiling, laughing, running among purple candles.
Little boxes of chocolates are left out for me to eat,
a water bowl and towel for me to wash away the soil
clinging to my face and hands.
Children run in circles, eating sugar skulls.
Mariachi bands roam the streets,
roaring songs to entice me to dance
with the other skeletons:
skeleton farmers, fishermen, doctors and priests,
all dancing, floating on paper maché flowers.
My son and his wife walk to the graveyard,
bringing photos and flowers. They cut down weeds,
spread a blanket over the grave, laying out a feast of
chicken in molé sauce, sweet rolls, and fine liqueur.
I eat until food pushes against my ribs.
I smoke cigars, swirl in puffs of tobacco and cedar,
see past friends wave to me, perched on their tombstones.
I hear bells every minute, calling me to return,
but I grow weary, my body not used to living.
My bones collapse into sleep,
assuming their familiar position of rest.
The earth swallows me whole—I slide into
my hollow between tree roots.
But as the sun rises and the people go away,
the music and aromas of last night
still cling to my bones
for me to enjoy in the year to come.

THE ATOMIC MUSEUM IN ALBUQUERQUE

I had never seen a nuclear weapon before
not even a replica as I saw that day,
a shell the size of a sofa,
the bomb named "Little Boy" dropped on Hiroshima.
My chest grew tight as if before a growling wolf.
I didn't want to get too close to
this bulging cylinder filled with enough power
to kill 100,000 people.

Earlier that day, I had seen faded army movies of Trinity,
the original test site, the countdown, the silence,
then a flash, the glowing mushroom cloud
distinctive as the markings on a black widow.
This was no Hollywood fantasy; it happened.
The explosion fused desert into glass,
completely vaporized the containing tower.
All this witnessed by a few who later partied all night,
their faces exuberant, but only weeks later,
they would witness the blast again,
the devastated landscape where once a city had been.
This was their accomplishment and the war was won.

But the museum did not stop there.
The military sought ways to deliver the bomb
without losing men in the process.
I saw photos of bombs launched from rockets and mortars,
a few soldiers perilously close to the deadly cloud in the distance.
Then came the hydrogen bomb.
If I could not imagine more destructive power,
this bomb was 100 atomic bombs—I begged them to stop.
The cloud in the distance had grown impossibly large,
able to consume entire cities in a single flash.
But the bomb continued to gain new abilities;
it could be launched from battleships and submarines.

10

Finally came the ICBM, a missile able to reach across continents.
Outside the museum I stood before a missile
as big as a semi-truck with three trailers.
I was scared by its enormous presence
let alone the payload inside.
To think I could drive fifteen miles away
and still not escape its fury.
We have thousands like it stored
in secret bunkers awaiting our order.
How could anyone feel comfortable with this?

My fear did not subside for hours,
the fallout permeating my old naive self with
the reality of what we had done.
I was like the Japanese at Hiroshima, caught off guard,
not knowing what a nuclear weapon was.
After hearing an American plane had passed over them
and not dropped any bombs,
the Japanese signaled an all-clear.
This was just minutes before the plane came back
to open its doors.
They didn't know what was coming
and neither did I.

Hiroshima Museum of Art

Here among the gentle green-blue drops
of Van Gogh's *Garden*,
my skin scalds with prickly awareness
that where I stand
a skull-white blossom incinerated the sky.

On this spot, now sixty years later,
where the people of Hiroshima
planted an art museum
in the heart of the death zone,
even now I feel dread,
shock waves through my body.

I need the revelry of Chagall's *Vitebsk*—
fiddlers prance below a married couple
embracing, floating above their simple town,
the neighbors dancing in yellow.
But my mind flashes
to the *before* and *after*
models of Hiroshima:
lines of houses, schools, the city hall—
then the eye blinks—
skeletons on the inner eye.

Two women slouch in Picasso's heavy blue air.
Their downward gaze at an empty glass
is like those hovering on the edge of life
like the photos I saw of survivors:
shocked, blinded,
lying on their stomachs,
legs and back unrecognizable
in layers of melted flesh.

How desperate I am
to see Matisse's young woman, healthy,
sitting in a room of crimson wallpaper, smiling,
a book on her lap, peacefully drinking her solitude.

Soon I am in Peace Park
where cherry trees release streams of pink blossoms
before my weary eyes.
High above the bridges of the Motoyasu river
had flashed the lightning blast.
Now, on top of the memorial to children,
a young girl stretches her hands heavenward
for a light that heals.

Kyoto Graveyard

My road to the hilltop shrine is interrupted
by a city of tombstone obelisks,
white granite engraved with black kanji
standing against foothills of willow and pine.

I watch as families wash the markers
with bamboo buckets,
adorn them with irises,
and blow spicy incense into the air.

From the cemetery well,
I look up at terrace upon terrace
of stone monoliths
outnumbering the living.

Each marker holds generations,
all of their ashes dwelling together
in a narrow house.

Spirits from when Kyoto
was ruled by the shogun
may still wander these old highways.

Not far from here,
leap the red spires of the Kiyomizu temple,
the road taking the traveler higher and closer to the divine.

I wonder why death is so unwelcome in my heart,
why I seek to bury it
in a field in a foreign land.

Someday, I will just stumble upon it
like finding a graveyard
on the road to the next tourist attraction,
where busloads of faces
will descend upon the hillside,
looking for a place to stand.

The Path and the Shrine

I.

At the bottom of the hill, my friend and I look up
at the foreboding gate, the sisha, lion dogs,
guarding the path upward to the abandoned shrine.
Through the darkened tunnel of trees we climb,
and I am thankful to visit my childhood friend
who has settled in Japan.

In our youth, we played basketball after church,
but on this trip, I will go to Mass alone.
Somewhere along the many years apart,
he has stopped believing.

At the top of the hill, we see the shuttered shrine
still graced by a few woven thatch braids
hanging from the rafters.
Some still believe.

Behind every shrine is a path to something else, my friend says.
Minutes later, we are in a bamboo forest.
Wind knocks the tall poles together,
a battle of sticks cracking above our heads.
Fuzzy new shoots pierce through the fallen leaves
emerging like caterpillars, growing a foot a day.

I hope my friend has found a new spiritual place to occupy,
but the old bamboo snaps underneath us.
My friend wobbles one of the shisa guardians
only to see it is concrete, then snaps off a chip of claw
revealing a millipede nest. My friend falls back,
remembers the day he was bit on his knuckle
and his hand swelled up for a week.

II.

I like to think I have found enlightenment
in my religion, in the daily prayer candles I light.

But the next day,
why do I stare so longingly
into the Kotohira shrine where we go,
surrounded by tourists,
vendors selling udon noodles and tea cups.
I wonder how far my prayers reach
into the cool stillness of the inner chambers
where the gold-faced deity watches impassively.

White-robed priests float
between temples on elevated walkways.
These temples are rebuilt every century,
stacked high on the mountain.
Inside alleys of stone lanterns and pink azaleas,
tourists wash their hands ritually
in dragon fountains.

My friend and I offer a coin for a prayer,
clap twice, and bow.
Later, we sit for a while on the stairs,
away from the crowds, looking out on the city,
hazy, but full of potential.
Between us, I feel a new faith emerge
in the silence of the shade.

ZEN ROCK GARDEN

pebbles smoothly guide
every foot and foot treading
upstream to the source

islands chipped away
by incessant ocean swells—
hands washed before prayer

summit peaks puncture
a drifting cloud continent—
moonlight on crane wings

dry boulders across
a rapid stretch of river—
ink strokes on parchment

pilgrims meditate
atop each stone to the shrine—
azaleas bloom again

The Spanish Masters

The Spanish masters knew light,
the way it drapes over the exposed torso
sagging with wrinkles.
The raised hand is illuminated in copper air
washing over the face pulled into itself
as a hermit deep in a cave of muddy orange.
Even in death, the body of Jesus
radiates white
snatching the gaze of the man
hoping to remain unobserved in shadows.
The last thoughts of martyrs are held
still as the sheep grazing the dark edges
around the rays of heavenly visions.
That place we once knew is lit again
with a disturbing bronze
that speaks of the absence
of other figures to share in this warmth
that permeates even the heaviest blacks.
The last painting seen
is the last candle before sleep,
every figure brushed with hues of forgetting:
the eyes of the beggar,
the yearning of the woman at the river—
all is hidden again
inside the tolling bell towers of the mind.

Picasso's "Las Meninas"

I.

Obsessed with reinterpreting the past,
Picasso grabbed the central figures
from Velazquez's most famous painting:
daughters posing for a picture, a dog at their feet,
the man observing in the doorway.
From this, Picasso's eyes became diamonds
reflecting and refracting this image.
His brush slapped the archetypes around,
endlessly stretched, squeezed, contorted them,
as if from painting to painting
a different revolutionary possessed his brush.

II.

Standing up in a glass jar, a brush.
Inside the hairs of the brush,
the miniature girls posing,
the thin wire of a panting dog,
and the man watching from a tiny door frame.
On the coat of the dog, a million colors
Velazquez never considered: magenta, vermilion, chartreuse.
Inside these colors, a multitude of geometric forms:
trapezoids, parallelograms, diamonds.
Inside these forms, molecules of artistic compounds
stretching, squeezing, and contorting together
in unpredictable ways.
Inside these molecules, Picasso
alone in a room full of brushes.

III.

Head full of diamonds, every thought painful,
as the repetition in painting grinds.

Chairs transfigure into daughters,
the lamp into a sleeping dog,
the curtains a man watching.
Velazquez's face transforms into a watch,
then a plate, then a mirror.
Picasso stretches, squeezes, contorts
household objects
into useless, shapeless voices
that cry out from pools of color.

IV.

Eyeball of Velazquez explodes into diamonds.
Brush head size of the Milky Way
sweeps across the fabric of time
revealing an endless hall of daughters
reclining, posing for a million different pictures,
a coiling dog snake twisting around their ankles,
a giant man watching, standing in every doorway.
Everything is stretched, squeezed and contorted
into the smallest possible anteroom
where only a remnant of figures survive.

V.

In another age possessed by dreams,
Picasso locked himself in a canvas tower
with a brush made from Velazquez's eyelashes
and the figurines of daughters, a sleeping dog,
and a man standing in a doorway
whom he could animate by command of his voice.
They would squeeze and stretch and contort themselves
and he would paint their sufferings
which poured from their eyes like diamonds.
The wind ripped off sections of canvas,
taking them to distant cities
where artists awoke to a new world.

Monasterio de Juso

Climbing the curving mountain road,
I wanted a good picture of our monastery hotel,
its angled stone tower
pressed against jade clouds of trees
and blue-gray mountains.

On my way up, I pass an elderly man, a local,
sun-darkened, wrinkled face, a few stray gray hairs
swaying as he staggers forward with a cane.
I salute him with *buenos tardes.*
Five minutes later, I look back at him
and he is still hobbling, stopping
to point his cane at roofs and hedges.

As I reach my desired vista, I inhale the grand panorama
of tan villages sprouted on foothills,
sea foam meadows pouring down the slopes
between strokes of upright evergreen,
and yellow-green feathers of birch
rocking in the breeze.
Somewhere deep in the valley,
a dog barks.
Once in a long while, a car comes.
I can hear an engine a long way off,
like the approaching shore from a ship,
an elongated experience of anticipation.
Finally, the car passes
and it is quiet again.

I frame my picture of the monastery
and click twice, concluding my roll of film.
With my picture coiled in a dark place
like a ring wrapped in a blanket,
I head back to the hotel.

But on my way back, I pass the old man again,
still climbing toward the clouds on a crutch.
I imagine he could be out here for another hour,
admiring the jewel that is his home
while I will go back to write postcards.
I nod to him and he says *Señor* as I saunter by.
I am probably not the first
or last tourist he will see in his town,
looking to capture a snapshot of another life.
But his voice seems to welcome me,
his cane pointing to distant purple fields.
I realize the afternoon light on the hills
is so amazing today, we both want a witness.

POSTCARDS

Postcards are points of light:
momentary flashes of my trip to France
my friend may not get for a week.
When she does,
she imagines me hiking
the sunny hills of Provence
when really I sit
at a Parisian cafe, reading.

This is the world we live in:
everything we see has already happened.
The sunlight that touches our hair
has taken eight minutes to
span the cold water of space.
Even our friends and lovers,
we see as they were in the past,
the smile of their youth.

Maybe that's why we want to nestle
so near the ones we love.
We want to give those photons
so little distance to travel
that we can claim,
even if incorrectly,
we experience the moment together.

II. Picnic Under Trees

BLOSSOM DRIVE

Every March, the trees on my street turned luminously purple.
The wind blew blossoms into snowstorms,
the curbs covered in banks of pink petals.
Our newspaper published a route through nearby farmlands
past plum orchards in full bloom.
I decided to take this trek with my first love.
Such love is like laughing aloud during biology class.
You forget your discretion; you have found a happiness
you can't help but share with everyone.

She had long since returned my clothes left at her house,
but to her I was still
a comfortable pair of shoes she didn't want to throw away.
Just the two of us went; it had not been long since
we had gotten our driver's licenses.
On our previous dates, we sat in the backseat
while her mom or my parents drove us to the movies.

Suddenly, it was just us—I drove, she leaned next to me.
We saw white churches, fruit stands awaken from winter.
She spoke so intimately that day.
She told me how she had seen her father
for the first time in two years.
We stopped for cherry cobbler at a roadside farmhouse.

Every turn of the road revealed more crystal blue sky,
so unusual for Oregon, but we saw no fields of blossoms.
They were elusive, just beyond our vision
like the future. We both knew college was only a year away.
I was afraid, but in her, I sensed an impatience to grow up.
The oldest child, she felt she had waited long enough for adulthood.

We stopped for pictures of an old abandoned barn,
playing the parts
we had watched for years from the backseat.
She would point to an old school by the road
like we had been there before,
and picnicked under the twisting oak and evergreen.

As the sun set, we watched the giant field sprinklers
shoot brown water through the air.
We were far from home and would be late for dinner.
On the way back, there could have been several hills of blossoms,
but we didn't stop—
our eyes were tired of seeing things.
I took her home, and we went back to looking away
from each other in the school hallways.
The great banks of blossoms were swept away
by shovel and wind but not by my dreams
in which I swam all night in purple.

THE REDEMPTION OF DAVID

The first thing I thought when I saw him again
was his cruelty
to my best friend in college.
She wanted to break it off with him,
but he kept hanging around,
his dark form behind the stained glass doors
waiting for her after choir practice.
I was there when he reduced her to tears,
when he kept yelling: why are you trying to hurt me?
He told me to stay out of it,
asked me point-blank if I was interested in her.
I lied.

I wanted to live in her room of frogs and purple blankets.
She sought me out, shared her journals with me.
I kept reading and fell in love with the woman
who emerged from those pages.
Once she handed me a letter and said I couldn't read it
anywhere near her.
I walked to the top of the oldest campus building at night
looking out on the stream of orange running paths.
Seven pages into it, she said she had been *coerced* by him
on multiple occasions.
I didn't want to say the word she meant.
She said, before she met me, she walked the campus late at night
wandering outside those orange lights
hoping *something* would happen, *something bad*.
Instead I came. Sent by God, she said.
But I spent all my time binding the wounds he left behind.

Here he was
sitting in the church lobby again.
After the priests had told him to stop coming,
he had sold everything and moved to Switzerland.
Now he was back, holding in one hand
a newborn puppy,
its eyes barely able to open.
He nursed it with a milk bottle,
one drop at a time.
Where did he get all this tenderness?
All the ugliness of the past seemed to melt away
as I watched him nurse this helpless puppy.
I believed suddenly he would never let any harm come to it.
She had married a man who looked like me.
He had found tenderness.
What would I do? I had to choose.

LETTER TO ANDREA

In college you kept your distance
even as I kissed you;
your lips formed words you did not speak.
However, you could never stop discussing
Russian philosophy and music.
Your whole body became restless and excited;
during your soliloquies, I felt forgotten.
At night, I could never reach you by phone--
you had fled to the Music Building
to play Rachmaninoff.
Is this why I wanted you? To make love with you
soaked with Russia and its winter imagination,
I would become helplessly entangled in the music you play,
and feel the breath of Russian philosophers on my face.
Then maybe I would have understood what you see and feel
when you tilt your head away
dreaming a cathedral of chords.

I should have said many things to you,
but now I know your body was the entrance to another world
I have only seen in books, only heard second-hand.
I would be thrown like you into something I cannot understand,
Russian men crying over dead lovers.
You told me a story I cannot forget.
Your favorite composer, Rachmaninoff,
wrote a song called "Tears"
that makes you cry whenever you play it.
You do not understand why you cry.
Rachmaninoff wrote the song for a grieving friend,
whose lover shot himself right before his eyes.
He saw him fall to the floor.
When we were together, I saw you fall,
but I could not catch you:
you had already passed into a world I could not follow.

KISSING IN WINTER

From hours of kissing under blankets,
the pillows cradling our faces,
we emerged, red faced, warm-nosed,
into the drip-drop chilly freshness
of air cleaned by waves of winter storms.

The steady tock-tock of drops in gutters,
the swish of our boots in shallow puddles
speak softly of the wheelbarrows of water
unleashed by conveyors above.

Your red scarf wraps us cheek to cheek,
an intertwining of sweaters, coats and gloves.

We are a bubble of warmth and intimacy
floating through the crisp wet night,
a few residual kisses landing on my face,
then yours as I open your car door.

By the rhythmic slip-slop of windshield wipers,
and renewed pattering on the roof,
we smile, knowing winter gives
such wonderful excuses for staying warm.

TOUCH

The birch tree next to my apartment balcony reaches
       to touch my potted fern.
The huge disparity in size makes the gesture
like a seven-foot man reaching
       to touch a caterpillar.
Patiently, the tree directs its fragile tips closer
and one day, maybe even while I am asleep
       they will touch,
a sweet mingling of leaves.
What surprises me is how much I seem to forget
       this simple truth,
that living things want to be near other living things
for no other reason
       than to breathe each other's breath.

THE FERN THAT FELL

After a night of heavy wind,
I went out to my balcony to find
my potted fern fallen three stories to the patio floor.
I could see it down there, tilted on its side,
looking up at me like a little dog.
To rescue it,
I went downstairs knocking
on the appropriate door
in hopes the renter would smile at my story,
then return with my plant.
But no one answered the door.
I went out to the street, spied into the walled patio
and the back rooms. The drapes were surprisingly open,
but everything I saw appeared empty.
It was easy to assume no one lived there.
All I had to do was jump over the wall,
grab my fern, then jump over again—
less than a minute of trespassing
and I would have my plant back,
except I felt strange, illegal.
People passed me on the street as I deliberated.
Then I went home, but I could still see it down there,
looking up at me like a child in a playpen.
I pretended that I really did not give up that easily,
but I did. I shrugged,
said there was nothing I could do. I prayed for rain,
thought about dripping water down to it,
but it was only a matter of time
before its soil dried up, its fronds turned stiff.
At night, I dreamt it grew tall and stocky
even without my water; it grew as large as the trees.
It returned to me,
bumping its branches against my window.

EMPTY SPACES

Walking together in oak-shadowed meadows overlooking the Bay,
the grass is taller now, up to my thighs.

When we first went scuba diving,
you descended before me into opaque blue-black.
All I saw of you were tiny bubbles, one, then another,
and I went chasing after these signs
hoping to find you.

Wandering the quiet midnight streets,
I see an enclosed porch filled with lamps,
and I feel such terrible emptiness
knowing you never want to hold
another life inside you. The week we broke up,
you cried all night like a baby.

I insert you into memories.
The day I got laid off from my first job, you met me at the park,
and helped me fill my pockets with winter jasmine.
I still find golden petals in my coat
whenever I put my hands inside—and you know this space inside.

How gigantic the wind tunnel you showed me.
Our voices could never reach a wall. The redwood propellers
seemed they could alter the course of the cosmos.
Only a month later, the tunnel was closed forever.

The night you got the keys to your new townhouse,
you led me inside.
We kissed in the dark rooms, cuddled in the bedroom closet,
and every empty place felt so full of promise.

After our breakup, I snuck into your old apartment—
carpet and cabinets gone
like seeing the body of your cousin missing her face.
You were in your new house, now full of furniture, none of it mine,
no longer any empty places left in your life for me.

THE INTERRUPTION

The phone rings—
my dad chokes as he speaks—
my mom's in the hospital, something about
a terrible stomach ache that wouldn't go away.
She was driving home from a conference
through small towns without hospitals,
until finally she found one, after being examined,
the doctor gasped, demanded she be taken
to the emergency room for immediate surgery
to excise her appendix
which almost exploded inside her.
It could have been much worse. It could have been—
yes, it could have been, but it wasn't.

I fly home and so I am here.
She's sleeping now
in a hospital gown and looks grayer, frailer
than I've ever seen her, like a dried rose.
She's sleeping soundly despite a tube
snaking down her throat.

I know all this will pass,
this eerie, clean smell of the hospital room,
the quiet murmurs of other patients,
darkened rooms where the sick lie waiting
for their curtains to be spread open again.

In a month's time, she'll be back,
singing church hymns,
chopping peppers and zucchini for dinner,
and reading outside in the shade.

These moments by her bed,
where I whisper to her:
I love you. I'm here.
will disappear down the dark corridors of memory,
a brief interruption in our lives.

Except it feels like the day
when the disease will not be so easily treated,
when my mom will look at me
and I at her and know life ends. My dad too.
I don't feel ready.
Likely, I still have decades more with them,
but I can't escape the hospital bed either.
Who knows how much time any of us has left?

After visiting my mom, I go to the State Fair alone,
the yearly treat of tall spinning rides, raspberry scones,
and carnival games I loved so much growing up.
Everything is as I remembered: the cages of quivering rabbits,
the miniature gardens with ribbons on them,
except it is so much more expensive,
my twenties seem to dissolve in my hands,
and I notice how small, how energetic every child looks.

I buy a ticket for the carousel of swings.
I strap myself in, let my legs dangle as the machine lifts,
and my feet hover high above the crowds.
Minutes later, my cell phone rings.

The Same Day

A rock the size of a baseball
spins out at freeway speed
from under a gray truck and
whacks my right rear window.
I twist to see the damaged veins of glass,
then gunshot shatter implosion.
I swerve as if I'm under attack.
Cold January air whips in.
I stop at the nearest pay phone,
put the frozen receiver to my ear
to tell my friend I can't visit her today.

I arrive at work early to meet with my boss.
I walk across the empty parking lot.
He's at my desk waiting.
His boss comes with us
as we go up in the elevator
to the unfinished floors
of the building strangely quiet,
a hammer at the table where we sit.
They say I have fifteen minutes
to pack up all my stuff,
that I need to be gone before
anyone else arrives.
My boss who last week
shared a song with me
he wrote on his last trip to LA
looks at every piece of paper
I do and do not take.

All that remains of my window
is a pile of green glass
small as salt.
I buy duct tape
to seal up the gaping hole.
Even when I finish,
it looks like a black eye.
Shrills of wind
prying into the holes of the tape
remind me constantly
of the window I cannot close.

Walking Home from the Library

Emerging from the amber doors of the community library
with a backpack of nighttime novels,
I return to the confines of my campus flat
through the trick-or-treat neighborhoods.
The sun is gone, but the sky is still lit,
persisting like the smile of a good friend.
It is that wonderful time of day
when you turn on the first lamp,
the front curtains of every house glowing in candy corn brilliance.
It is that time when you hear the last shouts of children
as they jump off their big wheelers and go inside,
when cars pull into driveways,
and the autumn winds have not yet stirred the trees.
Far away, I hear a light mingling of voices and laughter,
the strained notes of a child practicing his trumpet.
As I walk by each window,
I hope to glimpse a pair of feet resting before dinner,
and I wish suddenly
to share the moment with someone,
though I know my own windows to be dark.

III. Cinnamon and Pepper Chai

THE PUMPKIN CARVER

The tree by your window aches.
Something crumbles, something snaps
   as a maple leaf falls.
      You did not want it to happen,
but a strange child cries under the tree
         because of the wind, that awful wind;
                  its rattling wakes you up at night.
We grow scared when we wake up,
      and it is still dark.
            We know blankets won't help,
         but we rely on them anyway.
To carve this pumpkin,
   is to infect it with wildness.
 Those rows of glowing pumpkins
         burn all night along the road.
               It's too early to be Halloween,
         but we forget
                  why it rains.

   We sit alone at night listening to the rain,
      a mystery novel in our lap,
         a cup of coffee in our hands.
   We think the sound peaceful,
      but we forget the rain-drenched bark,
         the pavement drains clogged with leaves.
We enjoy our sweaters, our overcoats,
      but stepping inside a friend's house for hot cider,
         we immediately look out again
               at what we leave behind,
      and we know
         the rain will be waiting for us.

You sit inside your car for a moment
        before turning the key.
            The rain speaks
                a kind of death on your windshield.
                        Puddles too deep for your boots
                grow murky and powerful.
                    You could sit here a long time
                                        without regret.

But you must go home again,
    and it's been there all along, that pumpkin.
You cannot forget the pumpkin,
        sitting on your kitchen table.
            You can only ignore it for so long—
                you cannot help but carve it.

ENTRANCE INTO THE UNDERWORLD

The face of the gargoyle in fog
is an entrance into the underworld.
We do not understand why we desire
to explore the tombs of dead men,
but we dream of descending

into catacombs with only a candle.
We need that kind of fear.
All our housing developments
have trampled over the dead.
We long to visit the old burials at night

where the old trees have grown stiff.
We are fascinated by old weapons,
pikes, rusted spears sticking up out of the ground.
Life was more brutal then,
telling myths around fires was the only truth.

Religion was still the rattling of bones in a bag.
The solitary man in the forest at night
could depend on nothing.
He slept with his axe in his hand,
a knife in the other.

He awoke to a pile of dead animals around him.
Out of wood and clay, he designed his own tomb
and dug elaborate tunnels with his knife.
If he saw another man,
maybe he would kill him,

or maybe they would dig together,
telling their own legends
and they would believe every word.
But they grew tired, their arms like stone,
their faces had grown thick with hair.

They could see the roots of every tree,
and they became caught.
They were pulled upward into the soil,
and the whole world became their tomb
and every tree their headstone.

GARGOYLE

Mist blurs the silent figure
clothed in faded moss.
Raindrops flow from the cleaved chin
splatter on his outstretched four-fingered hand.
The grinning lips betray a secret
so utterly horrible
all who look on this tortured face
must turn away
for fear they will see in this deformity
something of themselves.

These weathered hands know the silent,
gnawing deterioration inside every soul
that erodes the heart, makes brittle the bones,
sends men into sudden frenzy.
Like hornworts, this decay smothers
with nauseating spores, greedily expanding its control.
But this process is so torturously slow.
The victim can feel the pain of decay
gnawing away at his joy.

Someday, this stone enigma will be nothing
more than gravel crunching under passing shoes.
Then the malformed will vanish from garden terraces,
the midnight guards disappear from forgotten graveyards,
and this displaced, restless evil will pass over the land like mist
until it finds rest again, perched on the cathedral
hidden inside the dark recess of pride.

YESTERDAY'S NEWSPAPERS

I kept collecting yesterday's newspapers
thinking someday I would read them.
172 pounds
according to the recycling center scale.
172 pounds of articles I should read
stacked high enough I could eat off them.
There would have been enough
to construct a whole other me
made entirely of headlines,
a mummy
bandaged tight, sightless and yellow.
But today this other me is being mulched away
finally releasing the burden of so much ink,
a separation possible only by violence.

TRANSFIGURATION OF THE ORANGE

Orange peels unravel like mummy bandages
reveal its juicy soul squeezed tight.
The sacred secretions are stored in chilled jars
to be drunk by the Gods of Morning.

Once poured from the heavens,
these forewaters sank into underground root kingdoms
then ascended to the highest sun thrones,
nurtured a fetal flower unwrapping its gooey limbs,
then flashed pink wings that attempted to fly.

The idea of an orange swelled inside the blossom mind
until it broke out like a tumor
shedding wrinkled petal skin.

The original flower licked by prehistoric salamanders
still lurks inside this glowing princess goblet,
swirling with sugar oceans and white-finned sea dragons.

It falls into my hand,
          an entire world,
                    an entire history
flooding into my mouth,
washing away burial plots of my greatest desires
that reawaken and prick my tongue
in a thousand places at once,
a stinging pleasure that bleeds my self-restraint dry
until I am brushing my face with tarantula legs,
bitten by the orange desire to eat uncontrollably
to feel my brain bathe in ancient waters.

THE FOUNTAIN OF YOUTH

The famished explorer in red-crested breastplate
stumbled on a deserted dust-cracked square
surrounded by broken houses and pale grass.
The white-washed fountain, rising like a pillar of chipped faces,
contained only red dust.

The traveler collapsed, his pointed helmet
falling into sagebrush.

He awoke to brown faces, brown hands touching his beard.
His armor weighed him down.
He asked for water; they brought him salsa--
a big black jar
filled with tomatoes mixed with cilantro and chiles.
They put a corn tortilla in his hand.
He scooped up the salsa,
making sure he got the largest chunk of pepper.
He let it slide into his mouth before he bit
with sudden vigor, his eyes closed tight.
He chewed, felt the fountain spring alive in his mouth.
He smiled, praised God,
realized suddenly his death would never come.

ENCOUNTER

Bright green ferns crowd their way onto my path
as I hike through the coastal forest
with a bowl of chowder in my hand.
With each breath, I inhale seashells, sponges, and silt
which settle to the bottom of my lungs.
Ahead of me, a loud roar.
Behind me, a whisper. Everywhere, a conversation.
The ocean says so much I cannot understand.
Somewhere beyond these dense leaves, past these old pines,
not far from this footpath,
is the final clearing.
How can something so big be so elusive?

I look down, grasp the bowl so firmly
I feel I could crush its stone.
I remember finding it buried in the sand,
the ocean itself had carved out the center.
I feel the surge of foamy waters
in my chest, a center of swirling currents,
my bones, yielding to the tide.
A leaf brushes against my face and I look up.
My only desire is to be hollow.

Vernal Falls, Yosemite

Massive shattering of water.
The frothy roar hypnotizes.
I feel I'm inside a tsunami
watching the finger of God
pound down the granite firmament.

I imagine watching the time-lapse video
of a city street at night,
the car tail lights blurring into red lines,
buses shuttling past
like commuter trains of neon yellow
holding crowds before they arrive home
to sleep in countless beds
before they see the sun
leap up like a heartbeat.

The moon accelerates
like a phantom race car,
while the sun rockets like an orange dragster,
a frenzied sprint in which neither can gain ground.
Then the moon loses sliver by sliver
until only an anorexic face remains.

I'm still standing at the base of the falls.
I know I'll be back next year, the year after,
for a decade, as my face wrinkles, and my limbs ache.
My son will come with me, first only a baby on my back,
then a toddler in my arms,
a youngster at my feet, growing taller
foot by foot, gaining more hair, larger hands.
As I get weaker, he comes by himself
when I stop, when I can't, when I'm gone.
He will come year after year, sun-wrinkled himself,
brings his own son, soon dwarfing his dad,
generation follows generation
as father holds son who holds son who holds son.

IV. Bread from the Oven

HIKING THE WASH

Barely a month into my first semester of college,
two friends and I went hiking with the chaplain, Father Michael.
A week earlier, I had stumbled into his office crying.
He had watched with curious detachment
as I spoke of my philosophy teacher
who swore there was no God and said he could prove it.
I, with my green yearnings, had attempted to argue my professor
like a child trying to wrestle a man.
I fled, embarrassed at my toy chest of understanding.
After wandering the campus through my tears,
I knocked on Father Michael's door.
I swear within minutes
he had scissored my teacher's arguments to shreds.
I wished I could remember half of what he said.
I wanted to take him to class with me,
to pit him against my professor,
like a big brother against a bully,
but he suggested we go on a hike instead.

The place he chose, an hour drive from campus,
had a well-worn trail up a rocky bluff.
On the way down, he suggested we hike the wash
spilling off the mesa.
On this new path, our feet sunk into alluvial sand,
leaving footprints in the dry riverbed.
A sudden plunge forced us
to climb down boulders
into shallow pools hidden by the sun.
The afternoon heat bit into our necks
and clung to our ankles, as we jumped rock to rock.
We slid through narrow fissures,
that brushed dirt onto our backpacks.

About half-way down, Father Michael stopped
on a particularly flat stone, perched above
the final jagged descent into the desert below.
He had us sit down, as he took out
a vial of wine and medallion of wafers.
He celebrated Mass right there in the heart of the wash
where raging waters once flowed,
his arms outstretched, seemingly
touching the whole horizon of saguaro and sand.
He gave us each a verse of scripture to read aloud,
and our voices traveled farther than we ever imagined
deep into creosote and mesquite groves.
My previous ideas of religion:
of a priest standing at a pulpit,
of praying on kneelers,
were flooded away from me
as I felt the raw skin of earth under my feet,
a peculiar comfort in sweat and dirt, and
the feeling there were angels buzzing in the desert.

After Father Michael took us back, he shook each of our hands,
and said we should go hiking again, even without him.
I didn't understand at the time,
but my hiking life had just begun.

MAN OF LOAVES

My uncle, the priest, is always late for Thanksgiving dinner.
He always comes, visibly tired
from staying up all night baking bread,
dozens of miniature loaves,
he later sprinkled with holy water
then gave out to the crowd of children
who received the gift for their families.
What drove him to do something
no one expected?

It probably began with one loaf
then multiplied.
He kept thinking even at 2 AM
with a homily to write,
will this be enough?

He could see the one
who would get nothing,
knew that person as if it were himself.
No, God forgets no one.

Even though we already have rolls,
my mom uses his loaves first.
We pass them around, breaking open
his night's work with our hands,
and for a brief moment, he is calm,
letting his eyes close as we all begin to eat.

El Santurio de Chimayo

I stood on the spot where light once poured from the ground
and I didn't even know it, my right heel
dipping into the well of dirt, hitting a small shovel
meant for pilgrims to fill up jars with miraculous earth.
Everywhere I turned in this small chapel, I saw icons:
the Sorrowful Jesus; the Risen Jesus;
the Good Shepherd; the Virgin; the Lady of Roses.
As I raised my camera, I noticed photographs
tucked into corners—smiling faces of all ages—
babies, grandmas, newlyweds and graduates.
It was hard to imagine any of these people sick or dying,
which made me think of another set of pictures—
the same people in hospital beds, their faces pale,
their arms hooked to machines.
I hoped their prayers were answered.
But there were so many prayers in this room,
every available wall space taken, spilling into the next room.
Outside, hand-made crosses of twigs were wedged into fences,
a single photograph dangling from them.
What faith it took to put a cross on a hill
and think it made a difference.
The man who saw the original light come from the ground
dug with his bare hands, his hole large enough for his grave.
Instead, he emerged from the ground
with a glowing crucifix in his hands.
This is the miracle. Even if we are covered
with the dust of the earth, we will find life again.

The Prayer Room

Moving into my new apartment,
I decided to use my storage room for prayer.
I cleared away one corner surrounded by windows
shuttered with translucent blinds.
I created an altar by covering a stack of empty boxes
with a red linen cloth that tumbled light into twisting weave.
On top of this altar, I put a pot of violets, a white candle.
Above it I hung an icon of the Last Supper, Jesus himself
covered in brilliant blue cloth that flowed over the table.

The first day I prayed, I was in a lighthouse of the sun.
The light poured in so profusely, every thought
became illuminated as it circled toward the ceiling.
I felt the embrace of warm yellow throughout the day.
I wanted to keep visiting this room, this light, every morning,
but I became busy and made excuses.
The light required something from me;
I had to be present to enjoy it.
I was lucky if once a week I took the time.
I almost dreaded the intensity it required.

Then I stopped going altogether.
Every night, I knew the room was right behind my bed.
I placed my hands on the wall as if to push through it.
Every morning,
I knew the room was there,
the red weave, the warm yellow.
Every building I visited,
I imagined the room was just a door away.
I wanted so badly to slip inside
to feel the light on my face again.
Even at night, I imagined if I went inside,
the light would still be there
as if it had pooled all day
and I only had to open the door to release it.

Maybe I only imagined this,
but one night, I woke up suddenly
as if from a dog barking, and I went inside.
Street lamps lit the room a diffuse orange.
The air was still a bit warm from the day,
but I was happy to kneel in silence,
to have finally recaptured what was mine.

The day I moved,
I tried to pretend it was no big deal
to take apart this room,
lifting off the dusty red cloth,
to return the boxes back to use
filling them with books,
but I feared I had learned something dark about myself.
I had created my own heaven,
and I could not find time enough to visit,
even though it was only a few steps away.

THE LAST HOUR BEFORE MIDNIGHT

Father Miguel wanted to make sure we knew
what we were getting into.
"A man is going to die tonight," he said.
"No one will think less of you if you don't go."
I wanted to take a stand for something.
Father Miguel and his generation had protested wars at my age.
At some protests, he was even arrested.
I wanted to prove I was interested in more
than just studying books.

Nine of us went with him. It was already approaching midnight,
the sky shone like a chain link fence.
He spoke on the way, a lonely trek across desert,
the cacti appearing like men paralyzed in the moonlight.
He said, "This man has done horrible things.
He killed three people, one of them, a 7-year old girl.
But he was literally kicked into existence.
His father kicked his mother in the stomach while she was pregnant,
causing an early birth.
He spent many of his early years in a closet.
I do not say these things to excuse him,
but you should know more than the newspapers say."

We arrived at a roadblock of police cars;
a cop directed us to a circle of people already holding candles.
In the distance, I could see the dull orange glow of the prison,
and far down the road was another gathering
I could not hear, but I imagined the angry confrontation
if our groups should meet,
a clash of shouting voices and raised fists.

I held a candle; I watched as a loudspeaker
was passed from person to person, some angry, some sad.
One man berated us, saying nothing we did was enough,

that we had failed because it was still going to happen.
We could feel the approach of midnight; clouds hid the moon from sight.
We grew silent. Some people fell on their knees.
Far away I heard the single cry of a coyote.

I tried to pray
but all I could think was how I had been in class that afternoon,
how my probability professor filled the board with theorems,
saying we needed to prove them to understand them.
I saw myself raise my hand; I kept raising my hand,
as the professor erased the board again and again.

I heard whispers around me.
Father Miguel spoke into my ear:
"We got word that he's dead."
For a moment, I was back in the hospital
with my mom and my uncle
as we watched my grandmother die,
how mysteriously the breath leaves the body.
We all blew out our candles one by one,
then got back into the van.

On the ride home, our jaws were locked shut;
words were simply not there.
The world of my classes was beyond my reach.
I had been there when a man was killed in our name.
I wanted to stay awake, but the heaviness bound me, pulled my eyes shut.
I would gasp awake suddenly, only to fall back asleep,
unable to wake up, my hands clenched.

I do not remember how we got home,
only flashes of Father Miguel driving, his face unexpressive,
the headlights of the van barely denting the darkness of the desert.
Had I imagined the moon before? Was it still there?
I do not remember how I got back to my apartment,
how I got ready for bed, how I found my way back
to the world I knew before.

V. Berry Lemon Trifle

My Furniture is Smarter than Me

The problem with having a wishy-washy chair
is it might decide it doesn't want you sitting in it anymore
and dump you on the floor.

My sofa is always clamoring how it wants the right to vote.
We will not stand for your tyranny.
Who says a sofa should only be in the living room?
Why can't we also be in the kitchen?

When I sleep at night,
my bed whispers to me.
Enough is enough already.
Every night you lay on me;
I didn't ask you to.
Why couldn't you sleep on the sofa for a change?
Of course, if I try to sleep on the sofa,
the sofa says, *What do I look like, a bed?*

My lamp shades like to move while I'm reading.
"Hey," I say, "I'm trying to read here."
Hey yourself, I'm just trying to stay in shape.
Being a lampshade is a sedentary lifestyle.
Imagine if you sat on a light bulb all day.
You'd want to move your butt around too.

My coffee table laughs at the books I read,
What kind of crap is this?
The Bridges of Madison County? cough cough.
At least if you're going to pile books on me,
you could have a book on auto racing.
"You like auto racing?" I ask.
Sure, it says, *all coffee tables do.*

My hat rack tells me,
I'm so under appreciated!
All you do is throw coats on me!
I want hats, you hear, hats!!
It throws my coats on the floor.
Sombreros! Berets! Helmets! You hear me! Hats!!

My mirror tells me,
Whoa, there's a surprise.
Man, you look so different today.
I'm glad we had this little meeting, aren't you?
My God, is that what you're wearing?
You've been dressing in the dark again!

Listen, says my recliner, *you seem a bit depressed.*
I'm thinking life's got you down.
Why not recline for a while?
I settle into a comfortable pose,
but, suddenly, I'm tossed onto the floor.
Oops, says the recliner,
you must have hit the ejector button by accident.
The sofa cushions vibrate with laughter.

Even my refrigerator yells at me,
I want to be stocked full of beer!
I feel like such a sissy holding your diet pop
and garden burgers.

My kitchen table is at least nice to me.
It greets me in the morning,
but it also sings as I'm trying to eat my oatmeal.
It tells me, *I want to be an opera singer.*
"You can't do that," I say, "you're just a table."
Nonsense, it says, *if I can double in size to sit twelve people,*
I can certainly sing in falsetto.

Some days I don't know why I bother getting out of bed.

New Ruse of Dating

Are you loony? Do you wish you were in a relay?
To be truly hapless, you must loath yourself first.
Keep a postmortem outlook. Eventually, you'll find your true lout.
If you don't consider yourself a cad, no one else will either.
Yes, you are worry of love.

Where are all the illegible basket cases?
Take a class where menaces of the opposite sex are likely to be pressing.
Onion dating is the new hot way to meet sinkers.
Another waylay is to walk your dog and meet other pest lovers.
The goaded rule of meeting someone gray: Never fear regression.

How do you make the fierce move?
Try to avoid stupid pick-up lies.
It's impotent to just be yourself, only more confounded.
Women should learn how to flit, and laughing at his jolts never hurts.
Stand clueless together and see if there is any mutual attacking.

On a first date, just enjoin yourself and try to relapse.
You need to learn how to make a good first implosion.
Always smite a lot and remember your table manures.
At the end of a date, don't ever mother "When will I see you
aghast?"
Avoid having sex too swoon as that will only cloud your junk mail.

How do you know if you've found a key perk?
Does this person make you feel spacey?
Do you look forward to the tirade you will spew together?
Can you imagine spending the rest of your life with this prison?
If not, then maybe you should just keep on looping.

CARRIE

You buy soap at 7-11.
Look, there's the girl who's dating the man in her closet.
You know, the man with the enthusiastic chest hair.
Some day, that hair will grow out and cover the world!
Trust me, trust me, trust me—
the girl you see in the photo is me.
My brother once came out of the kitchen
with a great big white glob on his plate.
I knew it was whipped cream
but he swore it was mayonnaise.
You just seem to bring out the weirdness in him.
You have weird handwriting.
Sometimes you write Carrie and sometimes you write CArrie.
You put capital letters right in the middle of a wOrd.
Your neck ranks high in biteability.
What! I think you spelled that wrong.
Excuse me, I don't think we've met before.
Yes, we have. Your major is Education, but it used to be Engineering.
As a child you used to hide your vegetables in the couch.
We had a class together, and I sat right behind you everyday.
Don't you remember?
Most people go to 7-11 to buy pop,
and maybe as an afterthought will pick up a bar of soap.
But you went to 7-11 with the explicit purpose to buy soap.
Do they sell Puffs there too? Debbie wants to know.
Why are there different shoe sizes for men and women?
A size 4 women's shoe is a lot smaller than a size 4 men's shoe.
Everything would be much simpler if it were all equal.
But then, women would never get out of children's sizes.
Did you know that men designed high heels, hosiery and mini-skirts?
All part of that male domination and subordination of women.
You know the only purpose of man
is to impregnate as many women as possible,
to wipe out all other men's DNA.

Excuse me, but that is ridiculous.
You're going to be single for a long time.
That's too bad because you are perhaps the epitome of the kind of person
I would like to marry.
Excuse me, maybe my English is not so good,
but what is this word "perhaps"?
Here try some V-8.
It tastes just like tomato soup, only it's cold.
Yeech!
Why are you taking a knife if you're only going to get a salad?
Those poor dishwashers—
it's because of you that they have to stay later washing clean silverware.
You should have seen the look of terror on your face
as your lips got sucked into the straw.
Somehow my entire spaghetti dinner slid into the milk cooler.
Your hair smells like peppermint.
Face it, you have schizophrenic hair.
You use banana shampoo?
Do the bottles come in bunches?
Are the bottles green when you first buy them,
but then do they get black spots over time?
Alright, at least I don't buy my shampoo in another state.
It's Duh-buque, not Day-buque.
That sounds strange on my tongue.
You know I can't whistle, or blow bubbles either.
I grew up on pudding; maybe that's why I'm so tall.
Hook me up with some water.
Wait up a minute—is this the same water as last time?
Yes, and you had better finish it or I'll use it to water my Chia-pet.

You know it is a great honor to wear my sweatshirt—
most girls just dream of touching it,
but you wore it.
Imagine the jealousy.
You know girls are just lining up outside my door.
Was that a knock?
You did that—you can't fool me.
You're funny.
You're cute.
I feel like I'm floating.
I wrapped up a bar of soap for you.
I even bought it at 7-11.
Did you miss me?

TERMS OF COOKING

BLANCH—to realize at a critical moment while making dinner that you're missing a key ingredient.

BOIL—to come home late from work and scavenge your pantry for anything quick and easy.

BUTTERFLY—to make up an excuse to leave early from a dinner party so you don't have to help clean up.

CRIMP—to worry obsessively about whether there are any toxins in your food.

DREDGE—to fill up a house with a disgusting odor such as raw squid.

FOLD—to find miraculously enough food to serve an unexpected dinner guest.

GARNISH —to stand behind your lover while she's stirring at the stove, and nibble on her earlobes.

GLAZE—to praise endlessly your friend's meal even though he overcooked everything.

GRATE—to stockpile groceries in your refrigerator for meals you always plan to cook, but never do.

JULIENNE—to organize a potluck in which everyone has to bring dishes that fit within your narrow criteria.

KNEAD—to drink one or more glasses of wine before attempting to cook a complicated recipe.

Marinate—to have a long, multi-course dinner with your lover, hoping the whole time you'll end up in bed together later.

Mull—to suffer night after night of the same leftovers made over a week ago.

Poach—to put so much hot sauce on your food as to render it inedible.

Puree—to steer dinner conversation away from any contentious topics such as religion, politics, or sex.

Sear—to insist repeatedly that it's your roommate's turn to cook.

Toast—to recline in a sleepy state after overindulging in rich food, often leading to dreams of your next great meal.

traffic city blues

i have a blues guitarist in my trunk.
  after shopping, i open my trunk and
           he's there inside, strumming his guitar,
     a cigarette dangling from his mouth.
    he hands me my groceries,
  then keeps on playing.
   now, when i get in a traffic jam
          he comes out of the trunk
    and plays boogie woogie on my car roof.
     in rush hour, a bass player's
          stomping in a station wagon next to me
         and on the other side is a drummer
   grooving in the back of a pickup. they jam
          for hours, improvising with the stream of honks.
     i can't even play my radio anymore.
 anytime i play pop music, i hear him
banging on my trunk, and he turns up his amp
      he's got with him in there.
he doesn't ask for much,
    an occasional bottle of bourbon
      or pack of cigarettes.
    once i stayed in the trunk
       with him overnight
         and i didn't even miss the sun.
       with him playing, there was plenty of room
  to stretch out, more than i thought.
it made me want to take up guitar
but he said no.

you can only have one blues guitarist
in the trunk at a time, he said.
one day,
i get in an accident and swerve
so the trunk's away from damage
but i take the brunt of the charge.
my whole front end is smashed
so i can't leave my car.
i can still hear the guitar, my guy
strumming, how sometimes we get the blues,
how sometimes the blues get us.

A Man like a Fish

Women are more likely to be. . .
Men suffer higher rates of. . .
Still, women only earn. . .
There's a crisis with men in. . .
Women suffer a loss of. . .
More often, men commit. . .
1 in 3 women are. . .
Every man feels he is. . .
Every year more women are. . .
Men should have more say in. . .
Women should have the right to. . .
Fewer men are going to. . .
There aren't enough women in. . .
Usually, it's the woman who. . .
Men only do one third of. . .
A woman. . . a man like a fish. . . a bicycle.
A woman is expected to. . .
A man can't ever expect to. . .
Men can't handle it if. . .
Women have too high. . .
Women still hold out for. . .
Men only want to. . .
Men never think about. . .
More and more women realize. . .
Men start to doubt that. . .
Can't women and men just. . . ?
What if men. . . ?
What if women. . . ?
What if women and men. . . ?

OCEAN BEACH, SAN FRANCISCO

It's time to say good night, but my girlfriend stays deep
inside our embrace, trying to recover from the pain
of another day, of vessels shattering inside her,
with another work day just hours away.
I feel the softness of her neck as we sit in my car.
She leans over, whispers, *Let's go to beach.*
I feel the cold face of night on the other side
of my car window, but I say yes anyway.

We pour down the streets toward the ocean
like fog in reverse, spilling past houses
draped and darkened for the night,
only a few lonely headlights burn past us.

We arrive at the great swells, startling white under the moon.
I park at the overlook--the perfect view
across an invisible continent of ocean,
traces of ghostly waves running toward the shore.
Sweat beads slide between fingers as we hold hands,
and gusts break across our windshield,
that great movement inside, larger than worry,
more powerful than fear or anxiety.

We feel that choir of force wash over us,
across the tired city.
We are a boat hovering near the coast,
a shimmer in the dark. As we embrace,
the street lamps become lighthouses on the ridge
beckoning through wind and wave, calling us home.

BUTTERFLIES

The butterfly is a symbol of joy, you say,
as we watch two shining Monarchs chase and twirl
on breezes above the fragrance garden of
lavender, myrtle, and a tangy lemon leaf
named after you.
Wings emerge
as we float through botanical gardens,
finding secluded benches and time to sit.
Today, we laugh with the birds, but we both remember days
when our gardens were abandoned,
the rough skin of rocks on our fingers.
We bled late at night after our friends had gone home.

Across the many years, we heard the call of the bell
somewhere in the garden, knew it was ringing for us,
but we stayed away from the pain of chiming.
We slept in meadows surrounded by darkened pines.

We knew we were meant to be swept up into the wind of singing.
Why the wait? Why the long wait?
The truths of love cannot be told to anyone.
Today, after almost a year of love,
we feel so much weight
tossed off
from our shimmering bodies.
Today, we are butterflies.

www.ingramcontent.com/pod-product-compliance
Lightning Source LLC
Chambersburg PA
CBHW032029090426

42741CB00006B/780